BY STEPHEN MITCHELL

Poetry
Parables and Portraits

Prose
The Gospel According to Jesus

Translations and Adaptations
A Book of Psalms
Variable Directions: The Selected Poetry of Dan Pagis
Tao Te Ching
The Book of Job
The Selected Poetry of Yehuda Amichai *(with Chana Bloch)*
The Sonnets to Orpheus
The Lay of the Love and Death of Cornet Christoph Rilke
Letters to a Young Poet
The Notebooks of Malte Laurids Brigge
The Selected Poetry of Rainer Maria Rilke

Edited by Stephen Mitchell
Into the Garden: A Wedding Anthology *(with Robert Hass)*
The Enlightened Mind: An Anthology of Sacred Prose
The Enlightened Heart: An Anthology of Sacred Poetry
Dropping Ashes on the Buddha: The Teaching of Zen Master Seung Sahn

For Children
The Creation *(with paintings by Ori Sherman)*

Books on Tape
The Gospel According to Jesus
The Enlightened Mind
The Enlightened Heart
Letters to a Young Poet
Parables and Portraits
Tao Te Ching
The Book of Job
Selected Poems of Rainer Maria Rilke

A BOOK OF PSALMS

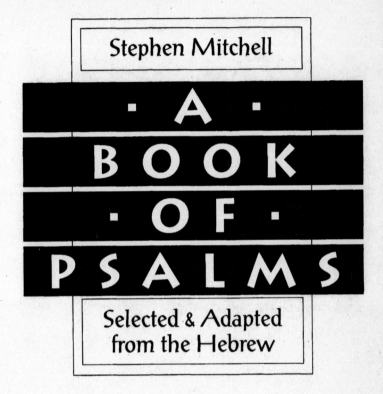

Stephen Mitchell

· A ·
BOOK
· OF ·
PSALMS

Selected & Adapted
from the Hebrew

Harper Perennial
A Division of HarperCollins*Publishers*

Some of these adaptations first appeared in the following
books: Psalms 1, 19, 104, and 131 in *The Enlightened Heart*,
three verses from Psalm 8 and three from Psalm 139 in *The
Enlightened Mind*, Psalm 147 and two further verses from
Psalm 139 in *The Gospel According to Jesus*, and Psalms 100 and
148 in *Into the Garden*.

First HarperPerennial edition published 1994.

Designed and typeset by David Bullen.

Library of Congress Catalog Card Number 92-54752
ISBN 0-06-092470-5 (pbk.)

04 05 RRD   14 15 16 17 18 19 20

To Elizabeth Vitale

CONTENTS

CONTENTS

CONTENTS

FOREWORD

The Hebrew word for psalm is *mizmór*, which means a hymn sung to the accompaniment of a lyre. But when the ancient rabbis named the anthology that we know as the Book of Psalms, they called it *séfer tehillím*, the Book of Praises. That is the dominant theme of the greatest of the Psalms: a rapturous praise, a deep, exuberant gratitude for being here.

The mind in harmony with the way things are sees that this is a good world, that life is good and death is good. It feels the joy that all creatures express by their very being, and finds its own music in accompanying the universal rapture.

> Let the heavens and the earth rejoice,
>   let the waves of the ocean roar,
> let the rivers clap their hands,
>   let the mountains rumble with joy,
> let the meadows sing out together,
>   let the trees of the forest exult.

Thus the Psalmists, in the ardor of their praise, enter the sabbath mind and stand at the center of creation, saying, "Behold, it is very good." This is the poet's essential role, as Rilke wrote in a late poem; when the public wonders, "But all the violence and horror in the world—how can you accept it?" Rilke's poet says simply, "I praise."

The praise is addressed to whom? to what? When gratitude wells up through our whole body, we don't even ask. Words such as *God* and *Tao* and *Buddha-nature* only point to the reality that is the source and essence of all things, the luminous intelligence that shines from the depths of the human heart: the vital, immanent, subtle, radiant X. The ancient Jews named this unnamable reality *yhvh*, "that which causes [everything] to exist," or, even more insightfully, *ehyéh*, "I am." Yet God is neither here nor there, neither before nor after, neither outside nor inside. As soon as we say that God is anything, we are a billion light-years away.

How supremely silly, then, to say that God is a he or a she. But because English lacks a personal pronoun to express what includes and transcends both genders, even those who know better may refer to God as "he." (Lao-tzu, wonderfully, calls "him" "it":

> There was something formless and perfect
> before the universe was born.
> It is serene. Empty.
> Solitary. Unchanging.
> Infinite. Eternally present.
> It is the mother of the universe.
> For lack of a better name,
> I call it the Tao.)

In the following adaptations, I have called God "him" for lack of a better pronoun. You should, of course, feel free to substitute "her" if you wish.

"Sing to the Lord a *new* song." My primary allegiance in these psalms was not to the Hebrew text but to my own sense of the genuine. I have translated fairly closely where that has been possible; but I have also paraphrased, expanded, contracted, deleted, shuffled the order of verses, and freely improvised on the themes of the originals. When I disregarded the letter entirely, it was so that I could follow the spirit, wherever it wanted to take me, into a language that felt genuine and alive.

The Psalms speak as both poetry and prayer. Some of them are very great poems. But as prayer, even the greatest poems are inadequate. Pure prayer begins at the threshold of silence. It says nothing, asks for nothing. It is a kind of listening. The deeper the listening, the less we listen for, until silence itself becomes the voice of God.

A BOOK OF PSALMS

Blessed are the man and the woman
    who have grown beyond their greed
    and have put an end to their hatred
    and no longer nourish illusions.
But they delight in the way things are
    and keep their hearts open, day and night.
They are like trees planted near flowing rivers,
    which bear fruit when they are ready.
Their leaves will not fall or wither.
    Everything they do will succeed.

· PSALM 4 ·

Even in the midst of great pain, Lord,
    I praise you for that which is.
I will not refuse this grief
    or close myself to this anguish.
Let shallow men pray for ease:
    "Comfort us; shield us from sorrow."
I pray for whatever you send me,
    and I ask to receive it as your gift.
You have put a joy in my heart
    greater than all the world's riches.
I lie down trusting the darkness,
    for I know that even now you are here.

Unnamable God, how measureless
   is your power on all the earth
   and how radiant in the sky!
When I look up at your heavens,
   the work of your fingers,
   the moon and the multitude of stars,
what is man, that you love him,
   and woman, that you gladden her heart?
Yet you made us almost like the angels
   and crowned us with understanding.
You put us in charge of all creatures
   and placed your whole earth in our hands:
all animals, tame and wild,
   all forests, fields, and deserts,
even the pure air of the sky,
   even the depths of the ocean.
Unnamable God, how terrible
   is our power on all the earth!

PSALM 13

How long will this pain go on, Lord,
   this grief I can hardly bear?
How long will anguish grip me
   and agony wring my mind?
Light up my eyes with your presence;
   let me feel your love in my bones.
Keep me from losing myself
   in ignorance and despair.
Teach me to be patient, Lord;
   teach me to be endlessly patient.
Let me trust that your love enfolds me
   when my heart feels desolate and dry.
I will sing to the Lord at all times,
   even from the depths of pain.

Lord, who can be trusted with power,
   and who may act in your place?
Those with a passion for justice,
   who speak the truth from their hearts;
who have let go of selfish interests
   and grown beyond their own lives;
who see the wretched as their family
   and the poor as their flesh and blood.
They alone are impartial
   and worthy of the people's trust.
Their compassion lights up the whole earth,
   and their kindness endures forever.

Unnamable God, I feel you
 with me at every moment.
You are my food, my drink,
 my sunlight, and the air I breathe.
You are the ground I have built on
 and the beauty that rejoices my heart.
I give thanks to you at all times
 for lifting me from my confusion,
for teaching me in the dark
 and showing me the path of life.
I have come to the center of the universe;
 I rest in your perfect love.
In your presence there is fullness of joy
 and blessedness forever and ever.

· PSALM 17 ·

Lord, listen to my prayer;
    hear me in my hour of need.
I am overwhelmed by my troubles
    and terrified by my thoughts.
Guide my feet on your path;
    don't let me stop or falter.
Teach me how powerful your love is
    and how insubstantial my fears.
Like the pupil of the eye protect me;
    hide me in the shadow of your wings.
Cover me with your mercy;
    rock me to sleep in the dark.
And let me, when I awaken,
    see nothing but the light of your face.

The heavens declare God's grandeur
and the radiance from which they arise.
Each dawn tells of his beauty;
each night shines with his grace.
Their testimony speaks to the whole world
and reaches to the ends of the earth.
In them is a path for the sun,
who steps forth handsome as a bridegroom
and rejoices like an athlete as he runs.
He starts at one end of the heavens
and circles to the other end,
and nothing can hide from his heat.

God's universe is perfect,
awing the mind.
God's truth is subtle,
baffling the intellect.
God's law is total,
quickening the breath.

PSALM 19

God's compassion is fathomless,
   refreshing the soul.
God's justice is absolute,
   lighting up the eyes.
God's love is radiant,
   rejoicing the heart,
more precious than the finest gold,
   sweeter than honey from the comb.

Help me to be aware of my selfishness,
   but without undue shame or self-judgment.
Let me know that you are always present,
   in every atom of my life.
Let me keep surrendering my self
   until I am utterly transparent.
Let my words be rooted in honesty
   and my thoughts be lost in your light,
Unnamable God, my essence,
   my origin, my life-blood, my home.

The Lord is my shepherd:
    I have everything that I need.
He makes me lie down in green pastures;
    he leads me beside the still waters;
    he refreshes my soul.
He guides me on the paths of righteousness,
    so that I may serve him with love.
Though I walk through the darkest valley
    or stand in the shadow of death,
I am not afraid,
    for I know you are always with me.
You spread a full table before me,
    even in times of great pain;
you feast me with your abundance
    and honor me like a king,
anointing my head with sweet oil,
    filling my cup to the brim.
Surely goodness and mercy will follow me

all the days of my life,
and I will live in God's radiance
forever and ever.

The earth belongs to the Lord,
 and everything on it is his.
For he founded it in empty space
 and breathed his own life-breath into it,
filling it with manifold creatures,
 each one precious in his sight.

Who is fit to hold power
 and worthy to act in God's place?
Those with a passion for the truth,
 who are horrified by injustice,
who act with mercy to the poor
 and take up the cause of the helpless,
who have let go of selfish concerns
 and see the whole earth as sacred,
refusing to exploit her creatures
 or to foul her waters and lands.
Their strength is in their compassion;

PSALM 24

God's light shines through their hearts.
Their children's children will bless them,
and the work of their hands will endure.

PSALM 30

I thank you and praise you, Lord,
   for saving me from disaster.
I cried out, "Help me, dear God;
   I'm frightened and have lost my way."
You came to me in the darkness;
   you breathed life into my bones.
You plucked me from the abyss;
   you healed me and made me whole.
You rescued me from despair;
   you turned my lament into dancing.
You lifted me up; you took off
   my mourning, and you clothed me with joy.

Sing to the Lord, you who love him;
   thank him from the depths of your hearts.
For though he may seem to be absent,
   in his presence is eternal life.
Tears may linger when night falls,
   but joy arrives with the dawn.

Therefore my soul blesses him
    with every breath that I take.
My song will thank him forever,
    and my silence will be filled with his praise.

PSALM 34

I will bless the Lord at all times;
   my lips will sing out his praise.
I will thank him for the love he has shown me
   and the clarity that gladdens my heart.
Sing out with me and thank him;
   be grateful for all his gifts.
Turn to him; let your soul
   feel his presence; oh taste
and see that the Lord is good;
   happy are those who trust him.

You who desire true life
   and wish to walk on God's path:
Depart from evil; do good;
   seek peace with all your soul.
The Lord cares for the righteous
   and watches over the merciful.
He is near when their hearts are broken;

when their spirits are crushed, he is with them.
And though they may undergo hardships,
he fills them with blessings in the end.

The wicked are lost in ignorance
    and enslaved by their own desires.
They chase after pleasure and power,
    with hearts clenched like a fist,
not even glimpsing God's justice,
    not seeing that they wander in the dark.
Their selfishness keeps God hidden,
    as thick clouds blot out the sun.

Your love is vaster than the sky, Lord,
    and reaches beyond the stars.
Your justice is firmer than the mountains,
    deeper than the ocean's depths.
You care for all earth's creatures;
    infinitely precious is your love.
All your children come to you
    and take refuge in the shadow of your wings.
They feast upon your abundance;
    they drink from the river of your joy.

PSALM 36

For with you is the fountain of life;
   in your light we see pure light.
Let all people know your will, Lord;
   let the wicked walk on your path.
Then we will hear earth's harmony,
   and your chorus will be complete.

Unnamable, unthinkable God,
Lord of the dead and the living,
teach us how transient we are
and how fragile is everything we love.
For all of us flash into being,
as insubstantial as a breath.
Our lives are a fleeting shadow;
then we vanish into the night.

And now, Lord, what do I wait for?
My only trust is in you.
Help me to give up my desires
and to let go of who I am.
You have granted me this brief existence,
which is almost nothing in your sight:
may I receive it gratefully
and gratefully give it back.
Turn toward me; touch my spirit;

PSALM 39

stay beside me, until
the moment when I must step out
into your final darkness.

• PSALM 40 •

I trusted you, Lord, and waited,
and you came to answer my plea.
You lifted me from the pit,
you pulled me out of the mire,
you set my feet on firm ground,
you made my steps unshakable.
You put a new song in my mouth
and gave me the power to praise you.
You opened me to the truth;
suddenly my eyes could see it.
And I knew you don't care about rituals
or the mummeries of religion.
The only thing that you want
is our whole being, at every moment.

Hold me in your embrace, Lord;
make me transparent in your light.
Grant me awareness; keep
my gratitude fresh each day.

PSALM 40

Let my song give blessing and insight
   to those who can't see for themselves.
And let your compassion always
   shine forth from the depths of my heart.

· PSALM 42 ·

As a deer longs for flowing streams,
   so my soul longs for you, O God.
I thirst for the living God;
   I ache for him day and night.
When will he fill me with his presence?
   When will I see his face?

Why are you desolate, my soul?
   Why weighed down by despair?
Trust in God; he will save you;
   you will sing to him with great joy.

My soul is heavy with anguish;
   my heart keeps longing for God.
I am lost in a sea of wretchedness;
   I drown in the waters of despair.

PSALM 42

The roar of waterfalls surrounds me,
   and the waves crash over my head.

Why are you desolate, my soul?
   Why weighed down by despair?
Trust in God; he will save you;
   you will sing to him with great joy.

· PSALM 46 ·

God is our refuge and strength,
    our safety in times of trouble.
We are calm though the whole earth trembles
    and the cliffs fall into the sea.
Our trust is in the Unnamable,
    the God who makes all things right.

Come see what the Lord has created,
    the miracles he does for mankind.
He puts an end to our wars
    and snaps our weapons like twigs.
He offers us his abundance
    and his peace, to the ends of the earth.
He whispers to the heart, "Be still
    and know that I am within you."

Our trust is in the Unnamable,
    the God who makes all things right.

· PSALM 51 ·

Forgive me, Lord, in your mercy;
    in your great love blot out my sin.
Lighten the weight of my offense;
    free my mind from its burden.
I am deeply conscious of my guilt;
    my sin is almost unbearable.
My heart is breaking with remorse
    and the shame of what I have done.

I know that you love the truth;
    teach me to live in wholeness.
Cleanse my spirit; wash me,
    and I will be whiter than snow.
Take away my guilt; wipe out
    every last trace of my sin.
Return me to myself and make me
    as pure as a newborn child.
Fill me with peace and gladness;
    let the bones that you crushed rejoice.

PSALM 51

Create a pure heart within me;
    let my soul wake up in your light.
Open me to your presence;
    flood me with your holy spirit.
Then I will stand and sing out
    the power of your forgiveness.
I will teach your love to the ignorant;
    the lost will find their way home.

Lord, open my lips,
    and my mouth will declare your praise.

The ignorant say to themselves,
    "All things are accidental;
there is no justice on earth,
    and after death there is nothing."
They think that they know; their minds
    move on the surface of things.
They don't perceive the deep patterns
    or understand who they are.
Thus they slip into selfishness
    or slide down into despair.

Let your light shine into them, Lord;
    let your wisdom transform their lives.
Let them realize where they come from;
    let their minds become spacious and clear.
Let compassion flow from their hearts,
    into the slightest of their actions.
Let them care for the weak and the wretched

and share their wealth with the poor.
Then I will burst out in thanksgiving
and rejoice in the power of your love.

PSALM 57

You are generous to me, dear Lord;
    you have taught my soul to trust you.
I have crept beside you and found
    shelter in the shadow of your wings.

My great joy, Lord, is to praise you;
    I will sing and awaken the dawn.
Wake up, my soul; wake up,
    music in the depths of my heart.
I will praise you, Lord, to all people
    and inspire them with my joy.
For your light is higher than the heavens,
    deeper than the mind can plunge.
You are truth itself, and your grandeur
    is spread over all the earth.

It is fitting to praise you, Lord,
    giver of all good things,
to thank you for your boundless mercy,
    which renews us and makes us whole.
Happy are those who find you
    and open themselves to your light.

Every day you appear to us
    and reveal your grandeur on the earth.
You create the hills and the mountains
    and set them immovably in place.
You silence the roaring of the seas;
    you calm the turmoil of the nations.
People to the ends of the earth
    are overawed by your wonders;
at the gates of morning and evening
    they stand up and shout for joy.

You care for the earth and nourish her,
    filling her rivers with your rain.

PSALM 65

You send down water to her furrows,
    making her ridges settle,
softening her with showers,
    and blessing her with new growth.
You make her soil rich and fertile
    and ready to bring forth fruit.
You crown the year with abundance;
    the earth overflows with your goodness.
The hills are covered with sheep;
    the valleys are clothed with grain.
The pastures fill up with lushness,
    and the meadows burst into bloom.
They shout their exhilaration;
    they sing; they are wild with joy.

PSALM 67

Bless us, Lord, with your peace;
    make your light shine within us,
so that your presence may be known
    and your love appear to all people.
Let all earth's nations honor you
    and all people shout out your praise:
Christian, Muslim, and Jew,
    idol-worshiper, agnostic,
Buddhist, Taoist, scientist,
    brown-skinned, yellow, and white.
Let wisdom speak in their hearts
    and justice light up their eyes.
Let all of them feel your presence
    and sing out in the fullness of joy.

Lord, how beautiful you are;
  how radiant the places you dwell in.
My soul yearns for your presence;
  my whole body longs for your light.
Even the wren finds a house
  and the sparrow a nest for herself.
Take me home, Lord; guide me
  to the place of perfect repose.
Let me feel you always within me;
  open my eyes to your love.

Happy are those who trust you
  and merge their will in your will.
They let go of all desires
  and give up everything they know,
until they finally enter
  the inmost temple of the heart,
where there is no self, no other,
  nothing, but only you.

· PSALM 90 ·

Lord, through all generations
    you have been our strength and our home.
Before the mountains were born
    or the oceans were brought to life,
    for all eternity, you are.
A thousand years in your sight
    are like yesterday when it passes.
You return our bodies to the dust
    and snuff out our lives like a candleflame.
You hurry us away; we vanish
    as suddenly as the grass:
in the morning it shoots up and flourishes,
    in the evening it wilts and dies.
For our life dissolves like a vision
    and fades into air like a cloud.
We live for seventy years,
    or eighty, if we are strong —

PSALM 90

years filled with pain and suffering;
    they pass, and we fly away.

Teach us how short our time is;
    let us know it in the depths of our souls.
Show us that all things are transient,
    as insubstantial as dreams,
and that after heaven and earth
    have vanished, there is only you.
Fill us in the morning with your wisdom;
    shine through us all our lives.
Let our hearts soon grow transparent
    in the radiance of your love.
Show us how precious each day is;
    teach us to be fully here.
And let the work of our hands
    prosper, for our little while.

PSALM 92

It is good to sing praise to you, Lord,
    and to thank you for all your blessings,
to proclaim your love in the morning
    and your faithfulness every night,
with the music of the human voice
    or the melody of my silence.
For you let me delight in your world, Lord;
    you make my heart sing with joy.

How great is your goodness, Lord;
    how unfathomable your justice!
It can't be seen by our eyes
    and can't be grasped by our thinking;
but every secret is told,
    every crime is punished,
every good deed is rewarded,
    every wrong is redressed.

PSALM 92

Though chaos rules on the surface,
   in the depths all becomes law.

And the wise flourish like palm trees;
   they grow like the cedars of Lebanon.
They are planted in the dark soil of God,
   and their leaves keep turning to his light.
Even in old age they bear fruit;
   they are green and supple and strong:
living proof that the Lord
   is just, and his way is perfect.

God acts within every moment
   and creates the world with each breath.
He speaks from the center of the universe,
   in the silence beyond all thought.
Mightier than the crash of a thunderstorm,
   mightier than the roar of the sea,
is God's voice silently speaking
   in the depths of the listening heart.

▪ PSALM 98 ▪

Sing to the Lord a new song,
   for his miracles renew us each day.
His justice is beyond comprehension,
   his beauty beyond all praise.
He opens the mind of the doubter
   and touches the fearful with his love.
Light is sown for the righteous
   and joy for the pure of heart.

Shout to the Lord, all creatures;
   burst forth in songs of thanksgiving.
Sing out with violins and harps;
   praise him with a chorus of voices;
with trumpets and the sound of the ram's horn
   make joyful music to the Lord.
Let the heavens and the earth rejoice,
   let the waves of the ocean roar,
let the rivers clap their hands,
   let the mountains rumble with joy,

let the meadows sing out together,
    let the trees of the forest exult—
in acknowledgment of the Lord,
    whose justice is always present,
whose truth hides beneath the surface,
    shining from the depths of the world,
whose law pulses in the atom
    and extends to the outermost star.

PSALM 100

Sing to the Lord, all creatures!
   Worship him with your joy;
   praise him with the sound of your laughter.
Know that we all belong to him,
   that he is our source and our home.
Enter his light with thanksgiving;
   fill your hearts with his praise.
For his goodness is beyond comprehension,
   and his deep love endures forever.

PSALM 102

Lord, answer my prayer;
    listen to my supplication.
Don't hide your radiance from me
    on the day of my desperate need.
Hear me when I cry out for mercy;
    hurry, send me your help.
For my days fly away like smoke,
    and my bones burn down to ashes.
Sorrow gives me no respite;
    anguish crushes my heart.
I am like an owl in the wilderness,
    like a hawk in the desert places.
All night I lie awake,
    like a sparrow upon a rooftop.
My food has all turned to ashes;
    tears are my only drink.

PSALM 102

My life is a lengthening shadow,
    and my days wither like grass.

But you, Lord, shine forth forever;
    you live beyond life and death.
Long ago you created the earth
    and made the heavens with your hands.
They will perish, but you will endure;
    like garments they will all wear out.
You will change them like clothes; they will vanish
    as though they had never been.

But you are forever the same, Lord,
    without beginning or end,
infinite in your compassion,
    fathomless in your love.

PSALM 102

You rebuild the desolate city;
  you bring the exiles back home.
You grant the poor your abundance;
  you guide the nations toward peace.
You hear the cry of the destitute
  and the sobbing of the oppressed.
You soothe the pain of the captive;
  you set the prisoner free.

Come to me too in your mercy
  and set my soul at peace.

PSALM 103

Bless the Lord, O my soul,
    and praise him, my inmost heart.
Bless the Lord, O my soul,
    and remember his unchanging love:
who forgives you for your wrongdoing
    and heals you of selfishness and fear;
who frees you from the darkest pit
    and crowns you with his compassion;
who pours light into you and makes you
    as fresh and vivid as a child.

The Lord gives himself equally
    to all men and women on earth:
he shines on the rich and the poor,
    the powerful and the oppressed.
He reveals his justice to all those
    who search to the depths of their minds.
The more they open themselves,
    the more they can feel his light.

PSALM 103

The Lord is joy and compassion,
  patience and unchanging love.
Higher than the heavens above us,
  vaster than space, is his love.
Longer than ten billion years
  will he wait for us to return.
As a father has compassion on his children,
  so the Lord has compassion on us all.
For he knows what we are made of;
  he remembers that we are dust.
Our lives are as brief as the grass is;
  we blossom like a flower in a field:
when a strong wind comes, it is rooted up
  and disappears from its place.
But the Lord's love is eternal,
  and his justice is everlasting.

PSALM 103

His law extends through the galaxies
   and into the atom's core.

Bless the Lord, you angels,
   echoing with the sound of light.
Bless the Lord, bodhisattvas,
   who have grown transparent in his love.
Bless the Lord, all creatures,
   through infinite dimensions of the world.
Bless the Lord, O my soul.

· PSALM 104 ·

Unnamable God, you are fathomless;
   I praise you with endless awe.
You are wrapped in light like a cloak;
   you stretch out the sky like a curtain.
You make the clouds your chariot;
   you walk on the wings of the wind.
You use the winds as your messengers,
   thunder and lightning as your servants.
You look at the earth—it trembles;
   you touch the hills and they smoke.
You laid the earth's foundations
   so that they would never be destroyed.
You covered the land with ocean;
   the waters rose over the mountains.
They fled at the sound of your voice;
   you thundered and they ran away.
They rushed down into the valleys,
   to the place you appointed for them.
You bounded them, so that they would never

come back to flood the earth.
You send streams into the valleys,
   and they flow out among the hills.
All the animals drink from them;
   the wild asses quench their thirst.
Beside them the birds of the air dwell,
   singing among the branches.
You water the hills from the sky;
   by your care the whole earth is nourished.
You make grass grow for the cattle
   and grains for the service of mankind,
to bring forth food from the earth
   and bread that strengthens the body,
oil that makes the face shine
   and wine that gladdens the heart.
You plant the trees that grow tall,
   pines, and cedars of Lebanon,
where many birds build their nests,
   and the stork on the topmost branches.

PSALM 104

The mountains shelter the wild goats;
   rock squirrels dwell in the cliffs.
You created the moon to count months;
   the sun knows when it must set.
You make darkness, it is night,
   and the forest animals emerge.
The young lions roar for their prey,
   seeking their food from God.
The sun rises, they withdraw
   and lie down together in their dens.
Humans go out to their labor
   and work until it is evening.
How manifold are your creatures, Lord!
   With wisdom you made them all;
   the whole earth is filled with your riches.
Here is the sea in its vastness,
   where innumerable creatures live,
   fish both tiny and huge.
Here sharks swim, and the whale

PSALM 104

which you created to play with.
All these depend on you
   to give them food in due time.
You open your hands——they gather it;
   you give it——they are filled with gladness.
You hide your face——they are stricken;
   you take back their breath——they die
   and return their bodies to the dust.
You send forth your breath——they are born,
   and with them you replenish the earth.
Your grandeur will last forever;
   eternally you rejoice in your works.
I will sing to you every moment;
   I will praise you with every breath.
May all selfishness disappear from me,
   and may you always shine from my heart.

Thank the Lord for his kindness,
  for his mercy endures forever.
Let those who were rescued from disaster
  acknowledge the mercy of the Lord.

Some lost their way in the desert
  and wandered in the barren wastes.
They were dying of thirst and hunger;
  their spirits melted within them.
So they cried out to the Lord in their trouble,
  and he rescued them from their distress.
He led them on a straight path
  till they reached an inhabited city.
Let them thank the Lord for his mercy,
  for the miracle he performed.
For he satisfies the longing soul,
  and he fills the hungry with good things.

Some sat in despair and darkness,
  shackled with iron chains.

Their spirits bent low with hard labor;
    they staggered under their burden.
So they cried out to the Lord in their trouble,
    and he rescued them from their distress.
He brought them out of the darkness;
    he freed them and broke their chains.
Let them thank the Lord for his mercy,
    for the miracle he performed.
For he bursts the bronze doors open
    and cuts through the iron bars.

Some were mortally ill,
    gripped by unceasing pain.
They sickened at the sight of food;
    they drew near the gates of death.
So they cried out to the Lord in their trouble,
    and he rescued them from their distress.
He sent his spirit to heal them
    and snatched their lives from the pit.
Let them thank the Lord for his mercy,

for the miracle he performed.
Let them thank him with songs of gratitude
and shout his wonders with great joy.

Some went to the sea in ships
and plied their trade on the ocean.
They saw the works of the Lord,
his miracles on the deep waters.
At his word a storm-wind arose
and churned the waves to a frenzy.
They were lifted high up, they fell
to the depths, they fainted in terror.
They reeled and staggered like drunks;
all their knowledge was useless.
So they cried out to the Lord in their trouble,
and he rescued them from their distress.
He stilled the storm to a whisper
and smoothed out the waves of the sea.

They rejoiced that the water was calm,
   and he brought them safe to their harbor.
Let them thank the Lord for his mercy,
   for the miracle he performed.
Let them sing his praise to all people
   and tell of his wonders with awe.

He turns great rivers into deserts
   and farms into barren lands.
He makes rich soil out of wilderness,
   and he fills the desert with streams.
He brings the hungry to live there;
   they build their houses and barns.
They sow fields and plant vineyards;
   their work makes the land rejoice.
He blesses them with abundance
   and enlarges their flocks and herds.
In times of desperate trouble,

he lifts them from their distress.
His mercy fills them with gratitude,
and they thank him with songs of praise.

Let all who are searching for wisdom
consider the great mercy of the Lord.

I thank God with all my heart
    for the gifts he has given mankind.
Uncountable are his miracles,
    immeasurable his love.
He has formed us in his own image
    and kindled his truth in our minds.
He has filled each day with his splendor
    and given us eyes to see,
hearts that can comprehend,
    spirits that stand in awe.
Also he has permitted us
    knowledge beyond our wisdom,
and has granted us, in our unripeness,
    the power to destroy the earth.
I praise his fathomless mercy
    and thank him for his difficult grace.
All beings perform his covenant
    and act out his primal law:
that whatever we reap, we have sown,

and what we give, we receive.
To know this is the beginning of wisdom;
to live it is the path of true life.

Happy are those who revere God
    and delight in doing his will.
Their children will be greatly honored
    and their grandchildren greatly blessed.
Abundance will fill their houses
    as gratitude fills their hearts.
They conduct their affairs with justice;
    their integrity cannot be shaken.
They give of themselves to the poor
    and share their wealth with the needy.
They are patient, cheerful, compassionate,
    generous, impeccably fair.
They harbor no regrets for the past
    and no worries about the future.
Their minds are centered in God,
    and they trust him with all their hearts.
They honor themselves, and are honored;
    they walk with their heads held high.
Their rising is like the sunrise,

and their light fills heaven and earth.
Their righteousness shines on all people;
their good works endure forever.

Praise the Lord, you who love him;
    praise him who is beyond praise.
Bless him, sing out his praises
    now and to the end of time.
Let all beings on earth and in heaven
    fill the world with his praise.
Praise him, praise him, the Unnamable,
    the All-Perfect, the Inconceivable,
who, higher than the highest heavens,
    stoops to the lowest of the low,
who raises the poor from the dunghill
    and lifts the wretched from the dust,
who grants them his infinite abundance
    and showers them with all good things,
who gives the barren wife children
    and overwhelms her with joy.

PSALM 114

When Israel went forth from Egypt,
   when a people of slaves was set free,
God was their only guardian,
   the Unnamable was their guide.
The Red Sea saw it and ran back;
   the mighty waters took flight.
Like rams the mountains leaped up;
   the small hills frolicked like lambs.
What made you run back, sea?
   Why did you take flight, waters?
What made you leap, mountains,
   and made the hills frolic like lambs?
The whole earth trembles and dances
   when the God of freedom appears,
who made the rock a clear pool
   and the boulder a bubbling spring.

PSALM 121

I look deep into my heart,
    to the core where wisdom arises.
Wisdom comes from the Unnamable
    and unifies heaven and earth.
The Unnamable is always with you,
    shining from the depths of your heart.
His peace will keep you untroubled
    even in the greatest pain.
When you find him present within you,
    you find truth at every moment.
He will guard you from all wrongdoing;
    he will guide your feet on his path.
He will temper your youth with patience;
    he will crown your old age with fulfillment.
And dying, you will leave your body
    as effortlessly as a sigh.

I rejoiced when I heard them announce,
   "The time of warfare is past.
No more will brother hate brother
   or violence have its way.
No more will they drown out God's silence
   and shut their hearts to his song."

Pray for peace in the cities
   and harmony among the races.
May peace come to live on our streets
   and justice within our walls.
With all my heart I will pray
   that peace comes to live among us.
For the sake of all earth's people,
   I will do my utmost for peace.

PSALM 126

When the Lord brought us back to Zion,
    we felt we were in a dream.
Our mouths overflowed with laughter,
    and song burst out on our tongues.
Every nation on earth said,
    "Look what the Lord has done for them!"
The Lord has done marvelous things for us;
    our hearts run over with joy.
He restored us among the nations;
    he brought us back from the dead,
like a dry riverbed in the desert,
    which swells to life in the spring.

Those who now sow in tears
    will reap with songs of thanksgiving.
Those who weep as they go out,
    carrying their bags of seed,
will come back singing with joy,
    carrying the harvest in their hands.

PSALM 127

Unless the Lord builds the house,
    it will not endure for long.
Unless the Lord guards the country,
    it will not be safe from danger.
Vainly you keep toiling and planning
    and worrying about tomorrow.
He gives joy to those who love him
    and blesses them with his peace.

Out of the depths, Lord, I call you;
    let me feel you even in this darkness.
Take away my affliction
    or give me the strength to endure.
If all our mistakes were indelible,
    which of us could survive?
But you have forgiven us, even
    when we cannot forgive ourselves.

I listen for you; my soul
    listens like a deer in the forest.
My soul waits more intently
    than a soldier watching for the dawn.
Answer me; open my heart
    so that I can wholly receive you.
And teach me that when I am ready,
    you will let this suffering pass.

PSALM 131

My mind is not noisy with desires, Lord,
  and my heart has satisfied its longing.
I do not care about religion
  or anything that is not you.
I have soothed and quieted my soul,
  like a child at its mother's breast.
My soul is as peaceful as a child
  sleeping in its mother's arms.

How wonderful it is to live
   in harmony with all people:
like stepping out of the bath,
   your whole body fresh and vibrant;
like the morning dew, glistening
   on the tiniest blade of grass.
It is God's infinite blessing,
   a taste of eternal life.

PSALM 136

Give thanks to the Lord for his kindness,
   for his mercy endures forever.
Give thanks to the Unnamable,
   for his mercy endures forever.
Give thanks to the Unfathomable,
   for his mercy endures forever:
whose miracles greet us each morning,
   for his mercy endures forever;
whose wonders flow past us each day,
   for his mercy endures forever;
whose light is brighter than the sun,
   for his mercy endures forever;
whose darkness is deeper than the night,
   for his mercy endures forever;
whose mind creates the whole universe,
   for his mercy endures forever;
who holds our lives in his hand,
   for his mercy endures forever;
who heals the afflicted soul,

PSALM 136

for his mercy endures forever;
who makes the wretched rejoice,
for his mercy endures forever;
who opens the hearts of the selfish,
for his mercy endures forever;
who leads the lost spirit home,
for his mercy endures forever.

Lord, you have searched me and known me;
   you understand everything I do;
   you are closer to me than my thoughts.
You see through my selfishness and weakness,
   into my inmost self.
There is not one corner of my mind
   that you do not know completely.
You are present before me, behind me,
   and you hold me in the palm of your hand.
Such knowledge is too awesome to grasp:
   so deep that I cannot fathom it.

Where can I go from your spirit?
   Where can I flee from your presence?
If I take the wings of the morning
   and fly to the ends of the sea,
even there your hand will guide me
   and your spirit will give me strength.
If I rise to heaven, I meet you;

PSALM 139

if I lie down in hell, you are there:
if I plunge through the fear of the terrorist
   or pierce through the rapist's rage,
you are there, in your infinite compassion,
   and my heart rejoices in your joy.

You fashioned my inward parts;
   you knit me in my mother's womb.
My soul was not hidden from you
   when I was being formed in secret,
   woven in the depths of the world.
How can I keep from praising you?
   I am fearfully and wonderfully made,
   and all your works are marvelous.
Your eyes saw all my actions;
   they were written down in your book;
all my days were created
   before even one of them was.
How measureless your mind is, Lord;

it contains inconceivable worlds
and is vaster than space, than time.
If ever I tried to fathom it,
I would be like a child counting
the grains of sand on a beach.

Search me, Lord; test me
to the depths of my inmost heart.
Root out all selfishness from me
and lead me in eternal life.

PSALM 146

I praise the Lord with my whole heart;
   with each breath I sing to my God.
Happy are those who trust him
   and surrender their lives to his care.
He creates us in his own image
   and fills us with his compassion,
opening the eyes of the blind
   and lifting up those who have fallen.
His justice shines from the depths,
   hidden but always present.
Praise him for what you can fathom;
   for what you can't fathom, praise him.

How sweet to sing to you, Lord,
  and to thank you for all your blessings.
You rebuild what has been ruined
  and recreate what was lost.
You heal the brokenhearted;
  you are medicine for their wounds.
You lift up the afflicted
  and give them the courage to endure.
You count the myriad stars
  and call each one by its name.
Infinite is your power,
  incalculable your wisdom.
You scatter the snow like wool
  and sprinkle the frost like ashes.
You strew ice crystals like breadcrumbs;
  the earth becomes bitter cold.
You breathe warm winds and the ice melts;
  you blow and the waters flash.
You cover the sky with clouds;

PSALM 147

you send down your rain to the earth,
making grass grow on the hills
and plants to nourish mankind.
You give the wild animals their prey;
you feed the young ravens when they cry.
You delight in the power of the horse
and take pleasure in the legs of an athlete.
But most, you rejoice in a pure heart
and in those who let you shine through them.
You give them joy in your joy,
and you bless their loves with your love.
You bring your peace to their families
and grant them your infinite wealth.
You send your wisdom to their minds;
your light runs faster than a thought.
Above all others they are blessed,
because they can hear you speak
(though your love speaks in all people,
in the silence of every heart).

PSALM 148

Praise God in the highest heavens;
   praise him beyond the stars.
Praise him, you bodhisattvas,
   you angels burning with his love.
Praise him in the depths of matter;
   praise him in atomic space.
Praise him, you whirling electrons,
   you unimaginable quarks.
Praise him in lifeless galaxies;
   praise him from the pit of black holes.
Praise him, creatures on all planets,
   inconceivable forms of life.
Let them all praise the Unnamable,
   for he is their source, their home.
He made them in all their beauty
   and the laws by which they exist.

Praise God upon the earth,
   whales and all creatures of the sea,

PSALM 148

fire, hail, snow, and frost,
    hurricanes fulfilling his command,
mountains and barren hills,
    fruit trees and cedar forests,
wild animals and tame,
    reptiles, insects, birds,
creatures invisible to the eye
    and tiniest one-celled beings,
rich and poor, powerful
    and oppressed, dark-skinned and light-skinned,
men and women alike,
    old and young together.
Let them praise the Unnamable God,
    whose goodness is the breath of life,
who made us in his own image,
    the light that fills heaven and earth.

Sing to the Lord a new song;
  praise him with words and silence.
Praise him through all your actions;
  praise him in sorrow and in joy.
Praise him with music and dancing,
  with bodies moving in delight.
Let the wise sing out in their freedom;
  let the whole earth echo their song.
Let all God's creatures be peaceful
  and walk in the path of true life.

▪ PSALM 150 ▪

Praise God in the depths of the universe;
    praise him in the human heart.
Praise him for his power and beauty,
    for his all-feeling, fathomless love.
Praise him with drums and trumpets,
    with string quartets and guitars.
Praise him in market and workplace,
    with computer, with hammer and nails.
Praise him in bedroom and kitchen;
    praise him with pots and pans.
Praise him in the temple of the present;
    let every breath be his praise.

ACKNOWLEDGMENTS

In Psalm 92, I have taken lines 13-16 from Emerson and line 18 from Rilke.

I want to express my gratitude to Robert Hass and John Tarrant for their helpful suggestions. And to my agent, Michael Katz. And, as always, to Vicki.